Starting
'Macbeth'

by
Adrian Lockwood

Series Editor
Eric Boagey

AYLESBURY COLLEGE

LEARNING RESOURCES

CENTRE

Published by HarperCollins Publishers Limited
77–85 Fulham Palace Road
Hammersmith
London
W6 8JB

www.**Collins**Education.com
On-line support for schools and colleges

© 2001 Adrian Lockwood and Eric Boagey
First published 2001

ISBN 0 00 323091 0

822.33
MAC
SHA
18774

British Library Cataloguing in Publication Data
A catalogue record for this publication is available from the British Library.

Acknowledgements
The following permissions to reproduce material are gratefully acknowledged:
Text: Collins Alexander Shakespeare edition of *Macbeth* for the play extracts and references
Photos: The Bridgeman Art Library, p. 7; © Donald Cooper/Photo*stage*, pp. 13, 16, 21, 24, 28, 32, 34.

Whilst every effort has been made both to contact the copyright holders and to give exact credit lines, this has not proved possible in every case.

Cover and internal artwork by Paul McCaffrey and Nigel Jordan
Cover design by Ken Vail Graphic Design
Internal design by Jordan Publishing Design
Commissioned by Helen Clark
Edited by Rachel Normington and Kim Richardson
Production by Katie Morris
Printed and bound by Imago,
Hong Kong

You might also like to visit
www.**fire**and**water**.co.uk
The book lover's website

KEY

 5.1   cross-reference to the play *Macbeth*

 p27   cross-reference within *Starting 'Macbeth'*

(H)   activity suitable for homework

Contents

Index of references to *Macbeth*

Act and scene	Page number	Act and scene	Page number
1.1	11, 14, 31, 36, 43	3.4	6, 15, 23, 34, 35, 43, 48
1.2	14, 17, 18, 46	3.5	15
1.3	9, 13, 14, 17, 18, 19, 31, 32	3.6	15
1.4	14, 18, 19, 36, 48	4.1	9, 12, 15, 24–25, 43, 46–47
1.5	8, 14, 26–27, 38, 48	4.2	15
1.6	14, 43	4.3	8, 15, 33, 38
1.7	14, 17, 20, 27	5.1	15, 29–30, 34–35, 36, 43
2.1	5, 11, 14, 21, 35	5.2	15
2.2	14, 17, 22, 29, 40–42	5.3	15
2.3	8, 14, 39, 43	5.4	15
2.4	14, 37	5.5	15, 25–26, 43
3.1	12, 15, 32	5.6	15
3.2	15, 23, 36	5.7	15
3.3	15	5.8	15, 17, 33

Coverage of Assessment Objectives

Assessment Objectives	Page number
Shakespeare's presentation of ideas	6, 8–9, 34–37, 44
The motivation and behaviour of characters	6, 18–33, 34–35, 41, 44, 46–47, 48
The development of plot	5, 14–17, 25, 45
The language of the scenes	21, 26–27, 38–39, 45, 48
The overall impact of the scenes	40–42, 45, 48
The presentation of the scenes on stage	5, 10–13, 28, 35, 37, 40–43, 45

Getting started

Ed and Sanjay talk over their ideas on *Macbeth*.

Ed	Well, what did you think, Sanjay? Difficult?
Sanjay	Some of the speeches were, but I found that if you know what's happening and where it's happening it doesn't matter if you don't understand a few lines.
Ed	And the plot is really straightforward. The witches get it going, Macbeth murders King Duncan, more murders follow and Macbeth gets more and more desperate until he is killed in battle by Macduff and Malcolm takes over to restore order. Well, that's putting it simply. Which scenes did you find most dramatic?
Sanjay	Oh, the murder of Duncan. That was really tense. I saw it in the theatre and you could hear a pin drop. But why didn't Shakespeare show him doing the murder?
Ed	I don't know. Sometimes it's more horrible to imagine an event than to see it. Shakespeare lets you experience it through Macbeth's imagination in his speech beginning 'Is this a dagger which I see before me?', and in his feeling of guilt afterwards.
Sanjay	Banquo's murder is different – that's more action than words.

2.1 >

Ed	Yes. Dramatic in a different way. Macbeth got the murderers to do his dirty work for him this time, but he still couldn't escape his conscience. The scene when he sees Banquo's ghost shows that.
Sanjay	He didn't seem to have much conscience when he had Macduff's family murdered. That was just slaughter. They weren't a threat to him.
Ed	He was taking revenge on Macduff for deserting him. But by then things were getting out of control for Macbeth, in himself and throughout the country. He didn't care any longer. Remember these lines:

> I am in blood
> Stepp'd in so far that, should I wade no more,
> Returning were as tedious as go o'er.

	That sums it up. And that's his tragedy. He starts off as a man with a conscience and ends up as a man without one!
Sanjay	It was all the witches' fault, wasn't it?
Ed	I don't think so. They didn't tell him to murder the king, they simply predicted that he would become king. As Duncan's cousin, Macbeth could have been *appointed* king. It was his idea to murder Duncan, and Lady Macbeth made sure he carried it out.
Sanjay	She sure did! She seems to be totally without conscience.
Ed	Well, it's true she seems capable of dashing her baby's brains out, but she does have a bit of human feeling. She would have killed Duncan herself in his sleep only he reminded her of her father. And, in a way, her conscience catches up on her, first in the sleepwalking scene and finally when she takes her own life.
Sanjay	Never thought of that. At least Macbeth dies fighting.
Ed	Yes, but not much to set against all his crimes. I think Shakespeare makes you feel Scotland will be a better place when Malcolm takes over. And maybe all those disturbances of nature will come to an end too. Things will get back to normal… till the next Macbeth comes along! After all, the ten kings who ruled before Macbeth were murdered.

 Discuss… Ed and Sanjay's opinions

Do you agree with everything Ed and Sanjay say? What aspects of the play did they not talk about? You could continue the discussion.

Historical background

The source for *Macbeth*

Shakespeare's source for the plot of *Macbeth* was Raphael Holinshed's *Chronicles of England, Scotland and Ireland*, which was published in 1577. Holinshed's account of the reign of the 11th-century Scottish king was based on a number of different sources, so its historical accuracy is questionable. Shakespeare, however, wasn't too concerned with historical accuracy as he wanted to produce a play that would be both exciting and interesting on stage. He therefore made a number of alterations and additions to Holinshed's account. One of the main changes he made was to shorten the length of Macbeth's reign from seventeen years to a period of only a few months. Why do you think he did this?

King James and *Macbeth*

When Shakespeare wrote *Macbeth* – probably around 1606 – the reigning monarch was King James I. He was also King James VI of Scotland, one of a line of Stewart kings who, according to Holinshed's *Chronicles*, traced their ancestry back to the legendary Banquo. In deciding to write a play about Macbeth, Shakespeare was therefore delving into the king's family history and he had to tread carefully.

King James

The first performance of the play was given at Hampton Court before King James and his brother-in-law, King Christian IV of Denmark, who was descended from King Duncan. There were many connections between Shakespeare's play and his royal audience. Let's look at some of them.

Shakespeare changed many details of Holinshed's account.
1. Though Holinshed describes the invading forces as Danish as well as Norwegian, Shakespeare makes no mention of the Danes.
   Do you think he had a reason for this?
2. In the *Chronicles*, Banquo was an accomplice in Duncan's murder.
   Why do you think Shakespeare omitted this and made Banquo a 'good' character?
3. In the *Chronicles*, there are references to Duncan's 'slackness' and 'softness'.
   Why did Shakespeare make Duncan so saintly?
4. Shakespeare omits the ten years between the murder of Duncan and the murder of Banquo, when Macbeth is said to have ruled well.
   Why did Shakespeare do this?

King James wanted to instruct his eldest son, the heir to the throne, in the qualities a king should have and he wrote a book for him called *The King's Gift*. One important quality was to have a conscience. The other qualities are mentioned by Malcolm as 'king-becoming graces' when he tests Macduff's loyalty in the 'English' scene in the play.
4.3 *What are the qualities of kingship mentioned in Act 4 scene 3?*

5 November 1605 – Gunpowder Plot. If this plot had succeeded King James and both houses of parliament would have been blown up. The audience would have been reminded of this by Duncan's murder. James himself played an important part in detecting the plot and a medal was struck to commemorate his action. It showed a serpent lurking among flowers.
1.5 *Find where Lady Macbeth echoes this image in Act 1 scene 5.*

In the 11th century it was the belief that the king was appointed by God to rule his kingdom justly and wisely. He was at the top of a hierarchy in which every level had its place. To rebel against the accepted order was to bring about confusion and strife. The worst crime was to kill the king, for it would inevitably be followed by suffering and political chaos.
2.3 *What kind of unnatural events does Lennox report in Act 2 scene 3 after the murder of Duncan? Look at the language used as well as the events.*

King James was interested in witches – with good reason. As king of Scotland there had been a plot against him by alleged witches which resulted in mass trials and many executions. During his reign he had more women put to death for witchcraft than any other monarch. His book condemning witches, called *Daemonologie*, was published in England in 1603 and in 1604 a strict law was introduced forbidding witchcraft.

The Church also condemned witches as agents of the devil, with supernatural powers to perform wicked deeds like striking a person down with illness, disease and madness; creating fires, tempests and thunderstorms; bringing bad luck; making false prophecies – and even plotting murder! Shakespeare's audience would undoubtedly take the witches in the play seriously and see them as 'instruments of darkness'. *Which of these 'wicked deeds' has Shakespeare included in* Macbeth*?*

1.3 ▷

You will remember that Duncan makes his son Malcolm the heir to the throne. He could just as easily have appointed Macbeth, for at that time the king's eldest son didn't automatically inherit the crown. The system meant that there was a great deal of rivalry among contenders for the throne. James was proud of the fact that he inherited the crown by 'linear descent' – that is, it was passed down from father to son, which ensured more stability and peace.
Where in the play does Shakespeare produce a procession of kings which would eventually lead to the most important member of his audience?

King James didn't like long plays – he used to fall asleep.
No marks for answering this question: Why is Macbeth *the shortest of Shakespeare's four great tragedies?*

 ### Discuss Macbeth... *now and then*

Shakespeare's audience could have had a very different attitude to events in the play from the attitude of a modern audience. How might the two audiences differ over the following aspects of the play:
- the murder of a king
- the king appointing his heir
- bravery in battle
- ghosts
- witches?

On the other hand, what views would the two audiences have in common?

The Elizabethan theatre

The diagram of The Globe theatre below will help you to imagine what it was like to go to a performance of *Macbeth* in Shakespeare's day.

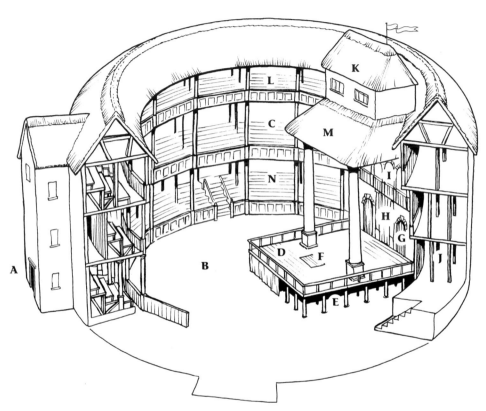

Key

A Main entrance

B The yard

C Middle gallery

D The stage

E The area under the stage known as the 'Hell'

F The stage trap, leading down to the Hell

G Stage doors

H Curtained alcove

I Gallery above the stage, used as required by musicians, spectators, and as part of the play

J Back-stage area (the tiring-house)

K The hut housing the machinery for lowering thrones etc and where thunder and lightning effects were created

L Upper gallery

M The 'Heavens'

N Lower gallery

The Globe theatre

> *The plays were performed in the afternoon, weren't they. Why?*

Because no artificial lighting was used, just daylight. And if it rained, some of the audience got wet! You would get to The Globe either by walking over London Bridge to the south bank of the Thames, or by ferry.

> *And how much was it to get in?*

It was a penny to stand around the stage in the yard. You'd be a 'groundling'. A seat in one of the galleries was twopence and an extra penny for a cushion. It was sixpence to sit in the lords' room overlooking the stage. You might be a bit squashed at a popular play and the audience could buy beer while the play was going on.

> *There wasn't any scenery, was there? So how did the audience know where the play was taking place?*

Shakespeare put a lot of information in the dialogue. If you look at the first scene, the witches tell us that they will meet again on the heath, at sunset, when the battle's done. This sets the scene for their encounter with Macbeth and Banquo. And because the play was acted in daylight and most of the action takes place at night, darkness is mentioned in the dialogue and indicated by 'properties' (props) A good example comes at the beginning of Act 2:

1.1 ▷

> *Enter Banquo, and Fleance with a torch before him*
> **BANQUO** How goes the night, boy?
> **FLEANCE** The moon is down; I have not heard the clock.

2.1 ▷

 ## Discuss... *References to time and place*

Can you find more examples of time and place in *Macbeth* that are indicated through dialogue and properties?

There's a musicians' gallery, but there wouldn't be much for them to play in Macbeth, would there?

There are 'hautboys' (oboes) when Duncan arrives at Macbeth's castle and when Macbeth is thinking about the murder. Trumpets often announced the entrance of a king and his party. There are songs in Act 3 scene 5 and Act 4 scene 1. And music when the witches dance. In Act 5 we have drums and 'alarums' for all the battle scenes. I think the musicians would be kept pretty busy!

What was in that little hut above the stage?

3.1

The turret house? That's where some properties were kept that had to be lowered onto the stage during the performance. When we first see Macbeth as king the throne might have been lowered, then pulled up again at the end of the scene.

And the trapdoor?

4.1

We can't be sure when it was used, but in the Apparition scene Macbeth says, 'Why sinks that cauldron?' Perhaps the cauldron sank through the trapdoor!

There are lots of properties and sound-effects in the play. How did the stage-manager produce them at just the right time?

Macbeth required a lot of artificial blood, as well as royal banners, the ingredients for the witches' cauldron, torches, dishes, drinking cups and a table for the banquet scene, branches of trees for Birnam Wood... not to mention sounds of horses' hooves and thunder and lightning! The properties were kept in the tiring-house behind the stage, where the actors put on their costumes.

Write... the stage-manager's notes

Imagine you are working backstage at The Globe theatre. Write out the notes you might have made for yourself for:
- all the sound-effects throughout the play; or
- the properties and special effects in the Apparition scene (Act 4 scene 1).

> Did boys play all the women's parts in Shakespeare's plays?

Yes. The plays were performed by a company of about sixteen men and boys, who were apprentices to the adult players (the word 'actor' didn't come in till later). It wasn't considered proper for women to act on the public stage, so boys took the female roles. In *Macbeth*, although the witches were played by men, they didn't even have to look like women because they were so weird. Remember Banquo's lines:

> *You should be women;*
> *And yet your beards forbid me to interpret*
> *That you are so.*

1.3 ▷

Do these witches look male or female?

 ## Write... a letter

Imagine you are living in London in the early 1600s and you decide to go to The Globe to see a performance of *Macbeth*. It is the first time you have been to the theatre. Write a letter to a friend who lives in the country, telling him or her:
- how you got to The Globe
- what it was like inside
- where you sat
- and what you thought of the play.

The plot

What does 'plot' mean? A simple definition is that it is the story. It also concerns the structure of the play; in other words, it is about the order in which things happen.

Below you will find a brief description of all the scenes in the play.

Act 1

1.1 Three witches plan to meet with Macbeth after the battle.

1.2 A wounded sergeant tells King Duncan how bravely Macbeth fought, defeating the rebels and the Norwegian forces. Duncan orders the Thane of Cawdor to be executed for betraying him and decides to give his title to Macbeth.

1.3 Returning from the battle Macbeth and Banquo meet three witches, who predict that Macbeth will be made Thane of Cawdor, then king, and that Banquo will be father to kings. Ross and Angus arrive and tell Macbeth he has been made Thane of Cawdor.

1.4 At the king's palace Duncan praises Macbeth and Banquo for their bravery in battle but makes his son Malcolm heir to the throne.

1.5 Lady Macbeth reads a letter from her husband which reveals the witches' prophecies. She is determined that he will be king and prays to the powers of darkness to strengthen her resolve. When Macbeth arrives she insists on the murder of the king.

1.6 Duncan arrives at Macbeth's castle commenting on how peaceful and pleasant it seems.

1.7 Macbeth is agitated. After much thought he finally decides that he cannot kill Duncan. Lady Macbeth accuses him of being a coward and persuades him to carry out the deed.

Act 2

2.1 While Macbeth is waiting for the bell to toll, an imaginary dagger appears before him pointing the way to Duncan. The bell tolls and Macbeth goes to murder Duncan.

2.2 Macbeth is distraught by the murder. He mistakenly brings the daggers with him instead of leaving them with the drugged guards. Lady Macbeth has to return the daggers herself.

2.3 There is a knocking at the castle door, which a drunken porter answers. Macduff and Lennox have come to wake the king. Macduff discovers the bloody scene and alerts the castle. Macbeth kills the guards. Duncan's sons fear for their lives and flee, Malcolm to England and Donalbain to Ireland.

2.4 Ross and an old man discuss strange events that have happened in the night. Macduff tells Ross that Macbeth is to be crowned king.

Act 3

3.1 Macbeth dreads that the witches' prophecies for Banquo will come true and tells two cut-throats to kill Banquo and Fleance.

3.2 Macbeth is restless and agitated and his wife tries to calm him.

3.3 The murderers kill Banquo but Fleance escapes.

3.4 Macbeth holds a banquet. In the midst of the celebrations Macbeth sees the bloody ghost of Banquo sitting in his place. Macbeth panics and Lady Macbeth asks the guests to leave.

3.5 Hecate meets the three witches and tells them off for interfering with Macbeth without her permission.

3.6 Lennox and another lord suspect that Macbeth is responsible for the murders of Banquo and Duncan. We are told that Macduff has fled to England to meet with Malcolm.

Act 4

4.1 Macbeth goes to meet the witches and demands to know more about his future. They make three further prophecies for him, two of which lead him to believe that he cannot be defeated. However, the first vision warns him of Macduff and a fourth vision shows that Banquo's heirs will be the kings of Scotland. Lennox enters with news that Macduff has gone to England. Macbeth decides to slaughter Macduff's family.

4.2 Murderers enter Macduff's castle and kill his wife and children.

4.3 Macduff shows his true loyalty to Malcolm at the English court. Ross arrives with the news about Macduff's family. Macduff is distraught and plans revenge.

Act 5

5.1 While sleepwalking, Lady Macbeth relives the murder of Duncan.

5.2 The Scottish rebel forces march towards Birnam to meet their English allies.

5.3 Macbeth, desperate and defiant, prepares for the final battle.

5.4 Malcolm's army camouflage themselves with branches cut from Birnam Wood.

5.5 Macbeth is told that his wife is dead and he reflects on the meaninglessness of life. A look-out tells him that Birnam Wood appears to be moving towards the castle. Macbeth realizes that one of the witches' prophecies is coming true.

5.6 Malcolm's army prepare to storm the castle.

5.7 The battle has begun. Young Siward is slain by Macbeth and Macduff goes after Macbeth to avenge his family.

5.8 Macduff confronts Macbeth. Macbeth says he fears no man born of a woman, according to the witches' prophecy. Macduff reveals that he was not naturally born, but delivered by Caesarean section. Macbeth is killed. Malcolm takes his place as king and proclaims peace for Scotland.

Shakespeare uses a number of devices in *Macbeth*, such as:

- Having the story focus on one main character, Macbeth, and showing his state of mind and how he changes
- Using aspects of the supernatural to grab the audience's attention
- Building up the tension in various parts of the play
- Bringing the play to a climax at the end with the battle between the two opposing forces.

Derek Jacobi as Macbeth, facing Macduff

 ### Discuss... *the plot*

1. The plot of this play centres around one main character. Retell the story from Macbeth's point of view, taking it in turns – like passing the baton – to follow it through to his final fight with Macduff.

2. A lot of the drama of the play comes from tension, particularly in the murder scenes, which Shakespeare has spaced out in Act 2 (Duncan), Act 3 (Banquo) and Act 4 (Macduff's family). How do these scenes differ? Which do you think could be most effective on stage?

3. *Macbeth* is not a whodunnit because we know who 'done' it! Yet Shakespeare still makes us want to know what happens next. What would an audience want to know after these scenes in the play:
    - The prophecies of the witches
    - The discovery of Duncan's murder
    - Macbeth being shown the apparitions?

Write about... *the plot*

Using the plot structure for reference, storyboard the play in the style of a comic. pp14–15

- The object is to tell the story in pictures but you can only use nine comic boxes. You must choose carefully which nine parts of the play to use to tell the story most effectively.
- Under each box give a brief summary of what is happening, such as 'Macbeth kills Duncan.'

 ## Discuss... *tragedy*

Tragedies such as *Macbeth* follow a similar pattern: the main character – the 'tragic hero' – suffers a fall from greatness, either through his own doing or through forces beyond his control, or a mixture of both. A tragedy usually ends in the hero's death. The audience may have mixed feelings about the tragic hero after his downfall. They may find the character unpleasant yet pity him at the same time.

Discuss what you think makes *Macbeth* a tragedy. Here are some opinions to get you started:

> Well, Macbeth is great at the beginning of the play – I like the way he unseamed Macdonwald 'from the nave to th' chaps' and fixed his head upon the battlements!

1.2

> But his downfall isn't as a warrior, it's because he starts off with a conscience and then gives it up...

> Are we supposed to feel pity for him at the end? I don't. He was a serial killer!

  ## Discuss and write about... *the turning point*

In the plot of a tragedy there is usually a 'turning point' for the central character. This marks the beginning of the character's downfall through his actions. Where do you think the turning point is for Macbeth? In pairs consider the possibilities below, then write down the arguments for the one you think was the main turning point in Macbeth's fall:

- The witches first tell Macbeth he will be king
- Macbeth is persuaded by Lady Macbeth to kill the king
- The murder of Duncan
- Macbeth faces Macduff in battle and learns that he is not 'of woman born'.

1.3
1.7
2.2
5.8

Are there any other possible turning points?

Characters

We study characters in a book or a play in almost exactly the same way as we study someone's character in real life – we think about what they do and say, and what other people think of them. In books and plays, of course, we rely on what the writer shows and tells us about that character. This includes the character's private thoughts and actions, which is an advantage we don't often have in real life.

Macbeth

Macbeth is a complex character and one of contrasts. His character also changes as the play progresses – what we see of Macbeth, Thane of Glamis, at the beginning of the play is very different to the kind of person he has become by the end.

 Before the tragic hero reaches the 'turning point' in the play, the story is often concerned with building up the reputation of the central character and establishing his greatness. It is as if the tragic hero must at first be raised up high so that his eventual downfall is all the greater.

First impressions

Some people say that first impressions count. What are our first impressions of Macbeth?

At the beginning of the play we are given a lot of information about Macbeth's reputation and how he is seen by others. Here are some statements that are made about him:

- **1.2** ● Sergeant: 'brave Macbeth—well he deserves that name'
- **1.2** ● Duncan: 'O valiant cousin! worthy gentleman!'
- **1.3** ● Ross: 'hail, most worthy Thane!'
- **1.4** ● Duncan: 'more is thy due than more than all can pay'.

  Discuss and write about... *our first impressions of Macbeth*

Read Act 1 scenes 2, 3 and 4 again.
1. What is our first impression of Macbeth? What has he done to gain his reputation?
2. Make a list of character points according to what the other characters have said about him.
3. Find a word, phrase or sentence from the text to support each character point.

Design... *a coat of arms*

Design a coat of arms for Macbeth which reflects the reputation he has gained. You may like to divide the shield into sections, and design something in each section which represents part of Macbeth's character at the beginning of the play, such as power or loyalty.

Too good to be true?

We are given a very favourable view of Macbeth by the other characters. However, Macbeth himself makes us question this view, for example by his reaction to the witches' prophecies. We are allowed to read Macbeth's mind with the use of the very handy 'aside' stage directions, which show when he is speaking his thoughts.

Here are some key lines from Macbeth's thoughts as revealed in his asides:

MACBETH [*aside*]   Two truths are told,
As happy prologues to the swelling act
Of the imperial theme...
This supernatural soliciting
Cannot be ill; cannot be good. If ill,
Why hath it given me earnest of success,
Commencing in a truth?...
If chance will have me King, why, chance may crown me,
Without my stir.

The witches' true descriptions of Macbeth (as Thane of Glamis, then Cawdor) are seen as the first parts of a drama that ends with Macbeth as king.

soliciting = egging on

1.3 >

MACBETH [*aside*] The Prince of Cumberland! That is a step,
On which I must fall down, or else o'er-leap,
For in my way it lies. Stars, hide your fires;
Let not light see my black and deep desires.

King Duncan has just announced that Malcolm will be his successor: the Prince of Cumberland was the recognized title of the heir to the throne.

1.4 >

  ## Discuss and write about... *Macbeth's hidden thoughts*

1. The two extracts above show a change in the way Macbeth thinks as the play goes along. What is the progression? How are Macbeth's thoughts in Act 1 scene 3 different to the way he is thinking in Act 1 scene 4 when he is before the king?

1.3 >
1.4 >

2. Draw a comic-strip version of the two scenes using thought bubbles to show the progression of Macbeth's secret thoughts from when the ▶▶

witches give their prophecies to when he meets the king. Put the quotations above into your own words, and try to show the contrast between what Macbeth is doing and what he is thinking.

A man of two minds

Macbeth is a very human character who suffers from a fatal flaw – ambition. But the fact that he isn't wholly a monster without a conscience comes across in his earlier soliloquies. (A **soliloquy** is a speech made when a character is alone on the stage and can speak his or her thoughts aloud.)

Macbeth's soliloquy that begins Act 1 scene 7 shows the inner conflict that he faces over the question of whether or not to kill Duncan. Here are some key lines from the soliloquy which take us through the stages of Macbeth's thoughts:

1.7

> MACBETH If it were done when 'tis done, then 'twere well
> It were done quickly...
>   But in these cases
> We still have judgment here...
>   He's here in double trust:
> First, as I am his kinsman and his subject...
>   I have no spur
> To prick the sides of my intent, but only
> Vaulting ambition, which o'er-leaps itself.

I have nothing to spur me on but ambition

1.7

 *Discuss... **Macbeth's inner conflict***

In pairs, talk about what each of the stages in the soliloquy shows about Macbeth's thoughts. Consider the following points:
- How is his thinking different at the end of this soliloquy from at the beginning?
- What, in Macbeth's mind, is stopping him from killing the king?
- What, by the end of the speech, does Macbeth recognize as being his weakness?

*Draw... **Macbeth's two minds***

Draw a picture of Macbeth as a 'Jekyll and Hyde' type character. One side should be drawn as a dark, secretive figure, and one side as the courageous warrior and respected thane. On the first side of the picture write down all the bad qualities associated with his character. On the other side write down all his positive qualities.

Discuss... Macbeth before the murder

Read Macbeth's soliloquy which ends Act 2 scene 1 ('Is this a dagger which I see before me...?'). This is Macbeth's last speech before he murders Duncan. His thoughts here are very different from those in the soliloquy from Act 1 scene 7.

In pairs, consider the following:
1. Why do you think Macbeth sees a dagger? What does it represent?
2. Look at the language in this speech. What kinds of images are present throughout? Make a list of these images.
3. Why has Macbeth's mind changed between the two soliloquies? What has happened in between?

Killing the king

At the beginning of the play we are told what a brave and ruthless warrior Macbeth is in defeating the rebels and the Norwegian forces. However, after the killing of Duncan he is in a panic. He brings the daggers that he has used for the murder back with him instead of leaving them with the drugged guards as he and Lady Macbeth had planned.

Roger Allum as Macbeth after he has murdered Duncan

Read Act 2 scene 2, where Macbeth has just killed Duncan. Look at the following lines from the scene spoken by Macbeth:

- 'But wherefore could not I pronounce "Amen"?/ I had most need of blessing, and 'Amen'/ Stuck in my throat.'
- 'Methought I heard a voice cry "Sleep no more;/ Macbeth does murder sleep"—the innocent sleep.'
- 'Glamis hath murder'd sleep; and therefore Cawdor/ Shall sleep no more—Macbeth shall sleep no more.'
- 'I'll go no more:/ I am afraid to think what I have done;/ Look on't again I dare not.'
- 'Will all great Neptune's ocean wash this blood/ Clean from my hand?'
- 'To know my deed, 'twere best not know myself.'

 ### *Write about... **Macbeth's reaction to killing Duncan***

Make a spider diagram showing what Macbeth is thinking and feeling in this scene. Use the evidence in the lines above and anything else you think is relevant in the scene.

 ### *Discuss... **Macbeth's fears***

Now that Macbeth has finally killed Duncan the path is clear for him to become king. But what is it that is haunting him? Working in groups of three or four, put the following statements into an order of importance for why Macbeth loses control after killing Duncan:

1 He is afraid of being found out.

2 He has lost God's blessing.

3 The murder was too horrific.

4 He has made the wrong decision.

5 He is haunted by his conscience.

6 He is paralysed with fear.

7 He is afraid that he will not be able to sleep.

8 He feels he was pushed into killing Duncan.

9 Someone might have heard him.

Macbeth, the king

Malcolm and Donalbain, Duncan's two sons, flee from Scotland fearing for their lives after their father is murdered. In doing so they make themselves look guilty of the murder and leave the way open for Macbeth to become king. Yet Macbeth finds little peace in being king. He has chosen the path of evil and finds that he cannot escape the consequences of his actions.

Read Act 3 scenes 2 and 4. The following lines from these scenes reveal how Macbeth feels:

- 'We have scotch'd the snake, not killed it.' `3.2`
- 'O, full of scorpions is my mind, dear wife!' `3.2`
- [*Seeing Banquo's ghost*] 'Thou canst not say I did it; never shake/ Thy gory locks at me.' `3.4`
- 'I am in blood/ Stepp'd in so far that, should I wade no more,/ Returning were as tedious as go o'er.' `3.4`

 *Discuss... **Macbeth's feelings***

Consider what the lines above tell you about Macbeth's feelings now he is king.

1. Divide your page down the middle into two columns headed 'Fears' and 'Wants'. Using your knowledge of the scenes and the quotations above, add notes to each of the columns. For 'Fears' include all the things Macbeth is afraid will happen and the things he does out of fear. For 'Wants' put down what Macbeth wishes for.
2. What does this list tell us about Macbeth's state of mind as king?
3. Why does Macbeth feel this way? What is it that he has realized about becoming king?

 *Write... **a secret letter***

Imagine you are one of Macbeth's personal servants who has been spying for Malcolm in England. Write a secret letter to Malcolm reporting on Macbeth's unusual behaviour since he became king. You could use these ideas and scenes to help you:

- Macbeth's solitude
- his secret meeting with the murderers
- the death of Banquo
- Macbeth's strange behaviour at the banquet in front of all the lords
- the hushed conversations with his wife.

Include your own thoughts, feelings and suspicions in your letter.

*Write about and discuss... **Macbeth as king***

Macbeth is a man who is tortured by his thoughts, fears and insecurities. But what kind of king has he become? In pairs, collect evidence from the text about Macbeth's reign as king, especially from Act 4 scene 3 when Macduff meets Malcolm in the English court.

Now discuss the following points:

1 What impression are we given of the state of Scotland under Macbeth's rule?

2 What methods does Macbeth use to rule over his people?

3 Macbeth is called a 'tyrant' in the play. What does this mean? Can you give some examples of real-life tyrants or dictators? What similarities can you find between their rule and Macbeth's?

Bob Peck as Macbeth

Macbeth is a man whose actions are often driven by insecurity. In Act 4 scene 1 Macbeth goes back to the witches. Determined that they will answer his questions, he demands to know what his future holds.

4.1

 *Discuss... **what Macbeth wants***

1 In small groups think about why Macbeth seeks out the witches again. What exactly does he want to know?

2 How do Macbeth's feelings change through Act 4 scene 1? How do each of the prophecies make him feel?

3 What does Macbeth mean when he says at the end, 'The very firstlings of my heart shall be/ The firstlings of my hand'? How does Macbeth say he is going to act?

4 What is his attitude towards the witches?

*Discuss... **how the prophecies turn out***

In pairs investigate how each of the prophecies turns out. (Go to Act 5.)
● Do you think the prophecies really helped Macbeth?
● How might his behaviour and actions have been different at the end if he hadn't gone to the witches?

'To-morrow, and to-morrow, and to-morrow'

By the final act of the play it is clear to Macbeth that kingship has not turned out the way he expected. Although he still remains confident because of the witches' prophecies, things are going against him:
● Malcolm, together with the English forces and other Scottish lords, has gathered a great army against Macbeth and surrounded his castle at Dunsinane.
● Lady Macbeth has given in to madness and eventually dies.
● Macbeth's rule is a bloody and tyrannical one. He has found himself trapped in a cycle of murder to maintain his position as king.

Macbeth's final soliloquy, in Act 5 scene 5, comes straight after he has been given news of his wife's death and that the enemy are gathering around his castle. The soliloquy gives us insight into Macbeth's mental state at the end of the play.

MACBETH To-morrow, and to-morrow, and to-morrow,   `5.5`
Creeps in this petty pace from day to day,
To the last syllable of recorded time,
And all our yesterdays have lighted fools
The way to dusty death. Out, out, brief candle!
Life's but a walking shadow, a poor <u>player</u>,   *actor*
That struts and frets his hour upon the stage,
And then is heard no more; it is a tale
Told by an idiot, full of sound and fury,
Signifying nothing.

 *Discuss... **Macbeth's state of mind by the end***   `5.5`

Read the soliloquy in Act 5 scene 5 and answer these questions:
❶ Talk about what Macbeth's ultimate conclusion about his life is. Where does he see his life going?

▶▶

2 At the beginning of the play, Macbeth was attracted by the idea of being king. How do you think he feels about kingship now?

2 At the beginning of the play, Macbeth was attracted by the idea of being king. How do you think he feels about kingship now?

3 Although Macbeth has chosen the path of evil, what do you think an audience might feel for him after this speech? Do we wholly despise him?

Lady Macbeth

Lady Macbeth is almost as important a character in the play as her husband. In the first half of the play she is the driving force behind Macbeth's success. Although both characters have the same ambition – for Macbeth to become king – they have very different personalities. It is this tension between the two characters that Shakespeare uses to make their scenes dramatic.

1.5 The first time we see Lady Macbeth is in Act 1 scene 5. She is reading the letter that Macbeth has sent her revealing the prophecy by the witches that he will become king. Look at the following key lines from the scene spoken by Lady Macbeth:

Glamis thou art, and Cawdor; and shalt be
What thou art promis'd. Yet I do fear thy nature;
It is too full o' th' milk of human kindness...
      Hie thee hither,
That I may pour my spirits into thine ear

       Come, you spirits
That tend on mortal thoughts, unsex me here;
And fill me, from the crown to the toe, top-full
Of direst cruelty...
     Come to my woman's breasts,
And take my milk for gall, you murd'ring ministers

[*to Macbeth*] O, never shall sun that morrow see!...
    look like th' innocent flower,
But be the serpent under't...
Leave all the rest to me.

Discuss... *what Lady Macbeth is thinking* 1.5

① What does the first quotation tell us about what Lady Macbeth feels about her husband? What does it tell us about their relationship?
② Which other characters in the play might use the kind of language Lady Macbeth uses in the second quotation?
③ Look at the last quotation. How does Lady Macbeth treat her husband once he arrives? What does this tell us about her character?

 ### Write about... *Lady Macbeth as a woman* 1.5

Look again at the second quotation on page 26. In Shakespeare's day people had very definite ideas about what it was to be male and female.
① Why do you think Lady Macbeth is in effect asking the spirits to rid her of her feminine qualities?
② Copy the following table into your books. Fill in the boxes to show the difference between generally accepted female qualities and what Lady Macbeth would replace them with.

Feminine qualities	What Lady Macbeth wants instead

The differences between Macbeth and Lady Macbeth

Before the murder of Duncan the characters of Macbeth and Lady Macbeth are clearly set against each other, revealing important differences in their personalities. At the beginning of Act 1 scene 7 Macbeth is indecisive: he is torn between his conscience and his desire to be king. By the end of his soliloquy (see page 20) he fears that he lacks the necessary strength to carry out his ambition and decides that the matter will go no further. Lady Macbeth's approach is very different.

1.7

p20

 ### Discuss... *the differences between Macbeth and Lady Macbeth* 1.7

Read Act 1 scene 7 (from the entrance of Lady Macbeth) and think about how the two main characters react to the same situation.
① What methods of persuasion does Lady Macbeth use on her husband? Try to find at least three ways in which she tries to get him to change his mind.
② Which of the two do you think holds more power? Put both their strengths on a scale of 1 (weakest) to 10 (strongest). Give a reason for your views.

Write about... *Lady Macbeth's physical appearance*

1. How do you think Lady Macbeth might be made to look to fit the characteristics she has revealed so far?
2. Thinking about style, motifs and colour, design a costume for Lady Macbeth that highlights her character.
3. Do either of the photos here fit your ideas about how Lady Macbeth should look?

Above: Cheryl Campbell as Lady Macbeth; below: Sara Kestelman as Lady Macbeth

Macbeth's behaviour is also contrasted with that of his wife after Duncan 2.2 > is killed, which reveals clear differences between the two characters. Macbeth's guilt and fear overwhelm him after he commits the murder and he is paralysed by this. Here are some of Lady Macbeth's reactions to her husband's fear:

- 'Consider it not so deeply.'
- 'These deeds must not be thought/ After these ways; so, it will make us mad.'
- 'Go get some water/ And wash this filthy witness from your hand.'
- 'Infirm of purpose!/ Give me the daggers.'
- 'My hands are of your colour; but I shame/ To wear a heart so white.'

 ## Write about... *the murder scene* 2.2 >

Fill in the following table to show the different reactions given by Macbeth and Lady Macbeth to what they have done. In the left-hand box write down quotations on separate lines that show Macbeth's actions and feelings. In the next box write down quotations or your own notes to show how Lady Macbeth reacts to each of these. In the final box say what this reveals about their characters at this stage in the play.

Quotation from Macbeth	Lady Macbeth's response	What this reveals about their characters
This is a sorry sight	A foolish thought to say a sorry sight	Macbeth shows signs of regret and weakness. Lady Macbeth is matter-of-fact and strong.

Lady Macbeth at the end of the play

In Act 5 scene 1 Lady Macbeth is being observed by her waiting 5.1 > gentlewoman and the doctor as she is sleepwalking and behaving strangely. This is also her final appearance in the play before we are told of her suicide.

 ## Discuss... *the sleepwalking scene* 5.1 >

1. Why do you think Lady Macbeth behaves in this way?
2. How does her behaviour here differ from that shown in earlier scenes? How has she changed?
3. Do you still feel loathing for her?

Write about... **Lady Macbeth's behaviour**

Choose one of the following pieces to write:
1. The doctor's medical notes observing what he has seen. Describe Lady Macbeth's behaviour, what she has said and what it might suggest to you. In your professional opinion explain what is causing her to behave in this way.
2. The gentlewoman talks of a piece of paper Lady Macbeth reads while sleepwalking. Imagine that it is written by Lady Macbeth herself: what might it reveal about her thoughts and feelings? Write the contents of the note.

Assessing the whole character

We have so far looked at Macbeth and Lady Macbeth's character in individual parts of the play. However, it is important to put all our evidence together to see how they change through the play. Only then can we get a fuller, more accurate picture of their character. Use the notes and observations you have made so far to help you with the following activities.

 Role play... **the career of Macbeth or Lady Macbeth**

In groups of three devise **either** five freeze-frame statues of Macbeth **or** three freeze-frame statues of Lady Macbeth that are to be used in a museum's Hall of Shame. The statues should trace how their character changes throughout the play.

  Write and act out... **'Scotland's Most Wanted'**

In groups of four or five write a script for a special episode of 'Scotland's Most Wanted', which presents the lives of Scotland's most notorious criminals. Include interviews with eye-witnesses and other characters, and dramatic reconstructions of key events and scenes.

Either present Macbeth **or** Lady Macbeth. In either case, show how their personality and character changed.

 Devise... **an audience opinion graph**

1. Plot a graph, such as that on page 31, which shows how our feelings towards Macbeth and Lady Macbeth might change as the play progresses. Use a different coloured pen for each character. ▶▶

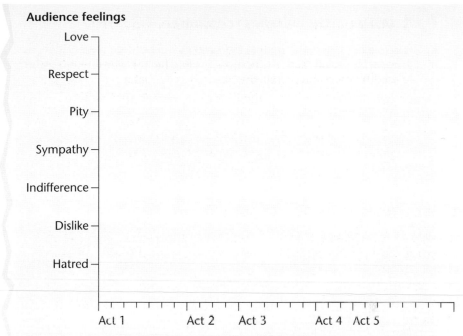

Audience feelings

Love —

Respect —

Pity —

Sympathy —

Indifference —

Dislike —

Hatred —

Act 1   Act 2   Act 3   Act 4   Act 5

2 What do the findings in your graph tell you about how the audience's feelings for Macbeth and Lady Macbeth change as the play progresses?

3 What are the main causes for the change in the way we feel about them?

Other characters

The witches

The play opens with the chant of the three witches. When Macbeth meets them he cannot help being won over by their prophecy that he will be king. However, the audience is left in no doubt that they represent the forces of evil and deception. Banquo warns Macbeth that 'oftentimes to win us to our harm,/ The instruments of darkness tell us truths/... to betray's/ In deepest consequence.'

  *Discuss and make notes on... **the role of the witches***

1 Think about what the role of the witches might be in the play. What do they do and how are they portrayed?

2 Make a spider diagram and include quotations from Act 1 scenes 1 and 3, Act 3 scene 5 and Act 4 scene 1.

3 Do you think the witches are fully responsible for what happens to Macbeth?

 Design... *the witches' costumes*

p9

In Shakespeare's day many people believed in witches (see page 9). An audience today would react to them in a very different way and a director would have to take this into account.

Design two different sets of costumes for the witches, the first for a production in Shakespeare's day, the second for a modern production.

Do you think these costumes are successful?

Banquo

The first time that we see Banquo he is at Macbeth's side, having fought with him in the battle, and he too is given a prophecy by the witches. It is interesting to see how Banquo's behaviour and character differ from Macbeth's.

Discuss... *Banquo*

1.3

❶ How does Banquo react differently to Macbeth when he too is given a prophecy? What is his attitude to the witches? What does this tell us about his character?

3.1

❷ Read the beginning of Act 3 scene 1. What is at the forefront of Banquo's mind at this point? What reasons might he have for not acting on his feelings?

Malcolm

Duncan names his son Malcolm heir to the throne. In many respects Malcolm is meant to contrast with Macbeth, particularly in the way they view kingship.

 *Discuss... **Malcolm***

1. Why do you think the play ends with Malcolm?
2. Look at Malcolm's final speech. What does he promise to do for Scotland?
3. Read Act 4 scene 3. What do you think Malcolm is doing by trying to trick Macduff into believing he would make a bad king? What does Malcolm think are the features of a good king?
4. Do you think Malcolm will be a successful king? Is there any evidence that he may not be?

5.8 >

4.3 >

Macduff

Unlike Banquo, Macduff leaves Macbeth after the murder of Duncan. Leaving behind his wife and family, he travels to England to offer help to Malcolm in his attempt to overthrow Macbeth. He learns that Macbeth has slaughtered his wife and children and it seems right that he should be the man who, at the end of the play, kills Macbeth.

 *Discuss... **Macduff***

1. Macduff had a dilemma: whether to put his country or his family first. He chose his country. Was he right?
2. How does Macduff compare with Banquo and Malcolm as a man who sticks by his principles?
3. There is a very human side to Macduff, which we see when Ross gives him the news of the slaughter of his family. What are your feelings for Macduff at this point?

4.3 >

Themes

A 'theme' is an important idea which is explored and developed through a piece of literature. *Macbeth* has several themes which are conveyed in two ways: through the plot and through the language, particularly in the use of **imagery** (verbal pictures: see page 38).

 p38

Themes in the plot

Ambition, conscience and guilt

Ambition is the driving force in the characters of both Macbeth and Lady Macbeth. It sets them on a path of murder and violence which eventually leads to their deaths.

Macbeth, however, has to do battle with his conscience; and once he has killed Duncan his feelings of guilt threaten to give him away.

Make notes on... *ambition, conscience and guilt*

1. Find the earliest example of Macbeth revealing his ambition.
2. When does Lady Macbeth first show she is ambitious for her husband?
3. What part do conscience and guilt play in Macbeth's actions after the murder of Duncan? Look particularly at Act 3 scene 4 and Act 4 scene 1.
4. Lady Macbeth's experience of conscience and guilt is different from Macbeth's. Make notes on Act 1 scenes 5 and 7, Act 2 scene 2, Act 3 scene 4 and Act 5 scene 1.

Cheryl Campbell as Lady Macbeth in the sleepwalking scene

Sleep, or rather the lack of it, plagues both of the main characters. To be able to sleep soundly is traditionally a sign of an untroubled mind or a clear conscience. After murdering Duncan, Macbeth states, 'Macbeth does murder sleep… Macbeth shall sleep no more'. It is no surprise, then, that Macbeth and Lady Macbeth have trouble with sleep.

  Discuss and make notes on… sleep

1. Discuss where in the play the issue of sleep arises. What kind of sleep do Macbeth and Lady Macbeth experience? What quotations can you find about sleep?
2. Look at Act 5 scene 1: what does Lady Macbeth's sleepwalking reveal about her state of mind?

5.1

Good versus evil, and the supernatural

The presence of evil is so strong in *Macbeth* that to the superstitious it is called 'The Scottish play', since to say its very name is supposed to bring bad luck to any production.

Macbeth's desires can only be achieved by acts of murder and violence. When he is king he rules by terror. His evil reign comes to an end when he is defeated by the forces of good, represented by Malcolm and Macduff and their armies. (Of course, there is also something in Macbeth's own character that leads to his doom.)

The role of the supernatural is closely linked with the theme of good and evil. In Shakespeare's time, ghosts, witches and supernatural visions were often regarded as a sign of evil, or of temptation by the Devil. Just like the belief in witches, the supernatural was a topic of great interest in those superstitious times, and it often featured in Shakespeare's plays.

  Discuss and perform… Macbeth's ghostly encounters

Look at Macbeth's first two encounters with the supernatural: the vision of the ghostly dagger, and Banquo's ghost at the banquet.

2.1
3.4

1. What do these ghostly visions tell us about Macbeth's state of mind in these two parts of the play? Do you think Banquo's ghost really came back to haunt Macbeth? How else might it be explained?
2. **Either** perform the dagger scene in two ways, first with and then without an actual dagger, **or** perform the scene with Banquo's ghost in two ways, first with and then without someone playing the ghost. What effect does the presence or absence of the ghostly vision have in either case?

Themes in the imagery

It is important to understand that it is also Shakespeare's language that sets the atmosphere and makes his ideas so vivid. The headings below list some of the main themes as revealed in the imagery of the play.

Masks and deception

A key theme in the play is the difference between appearance and reality. Macbeth and Lady Macbeth must play a game of deception and hide behind masks of innocence if they are to succeed in their ambition and avoid being discovered.

> For example, here is Duncan commenting on the traitorous Thane of Cawdor: 'There's no art/ To find the mind's construction in the face.' Further examples are in Act 1 scenes 5 and 7, and Act 3 scene 2.

Darkness

Shakespeare creates a murky, gloomy world through the imagery of darkness which runs throughout the play. Don't forget that a lot of the action takes place at night or in dark, shadowy places.

> For example, here is Macbeth after ordering the murder of Banquo: 'Come, seeling night,/ Scarf up the tender eye of pitiful day'. Further examples are in Act 1 scenes 4 and 5, Act 2 scenes 1 and 4, and Act 3 scenes 2 and 3.

Blood

Blood is an obvious theme in a play that deals with murder!

> For example, here is Lady Macbeth in the sleepwalking scene: 'Here's the smell of the blood still. All the perfumes of Arabia will not sweeten this little hand.' Further examples are in Act 1 scene 5, Act 2 scenes 1 and 2, Act 3 scene 4 and Act 5 scene 1.

Chaos and disorder

The opening scene of the play shows nature in turmoil with thunder and lightning. Scotland itself is being torn apart by the 'hurlyburly' of war. Macbeth defies the established order by murdering the rightful king, and his deed is paralleled in the strange and terrible events that occur in nature (see page 8).

1.1

For example, the witches end the first scene of the play with their chant, 'Fair is foul, and foul is fair'. Further examples are in Act 2 scenes 1, 3 and 4.

  *Discuss and write about... **themes in the imagery** of **Macbeth***

1. On a large sheet of paper, draw up a table like the one below. Find as many references as you can to these themes in the imagery of *Macbeth*. Write down quotations in the appropriate column, with the act and scene number. You can begin with the quotations listed above. Continue adding quotations to this table as you work on the play.

Masks and deception	Darkness	Blood	Chaos and disorder
There's no art to find the mind's construction in the face. (1.4)	Come, seeling night, scarf up the tender eye of pitiful day. (3.2)	Here's the smell of the blood still. (5.1)	Fair is foul, and foul is fair. (1.1)

2. The theme of deception is closely linked with the witches. Can you say how?
3. In the play darkness is both literal and symbolic. Design a stage setting for Macbeth's castle which conveys both these aspects of darkness.
4. In *Macbeth*, the imagery of blood is often linked with that of water. Find two examples of this and explain why the two are linked.
5. Read Act 2 scene 4 where Ross and the old man discuss the unnatural events that have recently taken place. How might these events be connected to what has happened in the castle?

2.4

 Design... a movie poster

Look back at your table of themes in the imagery. Design a movie poster for a film version of *Macbeth* which uses one of these themes in a dramatic manner. Use one of the quotations as a slogan or catch-phrase to promote the film.

Shakespeare's way with words

One of the reasons why Shakespeare's plays have remained so popular is his creative use of language. His inventive use of images and associations makes the speeches richer and more vivid – it's as if he is painting with words.

Figurative language and imagery

Figurative language occurs when a comparison is made between the thing being described and an image or verbal picture that illustrates it. The most common uses of this imagery are:

- **1.5** ● **Simile**, when a comparison is made using 'like' or 'as': 'Look like th' innocent flower'.
- **1.5** ● **Metaphor**, when 'like' or 'as' are omitted and one thing is said to *be* another: 'But be the serpent under't'.
- **4.3** ● **Personification**, when an idea or object is described as though it were a person: 'Did heaven look on,/ And would not take their part?'

 Discuss... *figurative language*

p37 Go back to the quotations you selected in the Themes section to find further examples of Shakespeare's use of figurative language to create verbal pictures for his audience. Have you included any similes, metaphors and personifications?

Prose and verse

Verse
Most of *Macbeth* is written in blank verse. It is 'blank' because it doesn't rhyme, but it is 'verse' because it has a regular pattern of ten syllables and five stresses to a line, though there are often variations. The witches, however, speak in rhymed verse with seven syllables to a line.

Prose
Prose is 'ordinary' writing, without any set rhythm or formal rules. It was often used by Shakespeare for comic characters and the obvious example from *Macbeth* is the porter's speech in Act 2 scene 3.

2.3 >

 *Drama... **reading verse***

1. Choose a speech in blank verse and read it in two ways: first sticking strictly to the rhythm and then putting a lot of expression into the lines but ignoring the verse form. What difference do you notice?
2. Now attempt a dramatic reading of the witches' verse in Act 1 scene 1 or Act 4 scene 1. Think first about voices, pace, rhythm and emphasis.

The language of expression

Shakespeare often uses striking words and phrases to convey a character's emotion or state of mind. In the passage below, Macbeth fabricates his outrage at the guards for supposedly killing the king.

MACBETH	The <u>expedition</u> of my violent love	*haste*
	Outrun the pauser reason. Here lay Duncan,	
	His silver skin lac'd with his golden blood;	
	And his gash'd stabs look'd like a <u>breach</u> in nature	*gap*
	For ruin's wasteful entrance; there, the murderers,	
	Steep'd in the colours of their trade, their daggers	
	<u>Unmannerly breech'd</u> with gore. Who could refrain,	*improperly*
	That had a heart to love, and in that heart	*covered*
	Courage to make's love known?	

2.3 >

 *Write about... **Macbeth's use of words***

1. Which words stress Macbeth's (supposed) love of Duncan?
2. Why are 'silver' and 'golden' appropriate words to apply to Duncan?
3. Which expressions emphasize the horror and violence of the murder?

In the director's chair

This is your opportunity to play the director of a production of *Macbeth*. You must remember that the actors will only have the script – it is up to you to bring it to life for the stage. Don't forget that the director has responsibility for all aspects of the production, from directing the acting and how the lines are delivered, to set and costume design.

In pairs, read the following extract from Act 2 scene 2. In this part of the scene Macbeth has just murdered the king and Lady Macbeth waits anxiously to hear what has happened.

2.2

MACBETH	I have done the deed. Didst thou not hear a noise?
LADY MACBETH	I heard the owl scream and the crickets cry.
	Did not you speak?
MACBETH	When?
LADY MACBETH	Now.
MACBETH	As I descended?
LADY MACBETH	Ay.
MACBETH	Hark!
	Who lies i' th' second chamber?
LADY MACBETH	Donalbain.
MACBETH	[*looking on his hands*] This is a sorry sight.
LADY MACBETH	A foolish thought to say a sorry sight.
MACBETH	There's one did laugh in's sleep, and one cried 'Murder!'
	That they did wake each other. I stood and heard them;
	But they did say their prayers, and address'd them
	Again to sleep.

LADY MACBETH	There are two lodg'd together.	
MACBETH	One cried 'God bless us,' and '<u>Amen</u>' the other, As they had seen me with these hangman's hands. List'ning their fear, I could not say 'Amen' When they did say 'God bless us!'	*'so be it' – making the prayer effective*
LADY MACBETH	Consider it not so deeply.	
MACBETH	But wherefore could I not pronounce 'Amen'? I had most need of blessing, and 'Amen' Stuck in my throat.	
LADY MACBETH	These deeds must not be thought After these ways: so, it will make us mad.	
MACBETH	Methought I heard a voice cry 'Sleep no more; Macbeth does murder sleep'—the innocent sleep, Sleep that <u>knits up the ravell'd sleave of care</u>, The death of each day's life, sore labour's bath, <u>Balm</u> of hurt minds, great nature's second course, Chief nourisher in life's feast.	*restores the unstitched cloth of care (soothes frayed nerves)* *a healing ointment*

If you are going to direct this scene there are several things you need to
take into account.

 ## Discuss... **the scene**

2.2

1. What is actually happening in the extract? Can you describe it in your own words?
2. Who seems more in control? Who is more emotional?
3. What is Macbeth's deepest concern?

Now that you have agreed on the basics, you need to consider the drama.
As a director or actor you have to consider ways in which you can build up
the tension. Here are some useful techniques:

Variations in pace

Pace is how fast or slow a
scene goes. It is also the speed
with which lines are read. For
example, reading at a fast
pace may indicate
nervousness. Reading at a
slower pace in a tense scene
may show the character's fear
and apprehension.

Variations in voice

Does the character's voice get
higher or lower, smoother or
broken up? Where one
character is cold and calm
and the other gets more and
more hysterical, the contrast
adds to the effect for an
audience.

Discuss... *the drama*

1. How does the length of the sentences at the beginning of the scene add to the tension?
2. What pace would you use in the scene?
3. What is Macbeth feeling? How would he speak and behave?
4. How would you show the essential differences between the two characters?

Read... *the scene*

1. In pairs, read the passage without any expression or emotion.
2. Now read it again, giving expression only to the questions.
3. Read it slowly, in whispers, then quickly and nervously. Think about the pauses.
4. What actions do you want to accompany the dialogue?
5. Now attempt a full dramatic reading, based on the exercises you have just done.

Write... *the director's notes*

As the director, write a set of instructions for the actors playing Macbeth and Lady Macbeth. Use ideas from your reading and include:
- how to behave
- how to move
- what actions to carry out
- how to speak certain key lines
- the emotions you want them to convey.

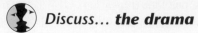 Direct and perform... *the scene*

In groups of three decide who will be the director and who will play the two parts. Rehearse the scene using the notes you have made and any other ideas you have. When you are confident enough, present your scene to the class.

Shakespeare's dramatic skill

As we have seen, a good dramatist knows how to build up tension, develop character, use expressive language and hold the audience's attention. Let us look at the various dramatic techniques that Shakespeare used in *Macbeth*.

Dramatic irony occurs when the audience is aware of something that the characters are unaware of – either in the plot or in what is being said. For example:

- We know from the first scene that the witches are going to meet Macbeth and will have some sinister effect on his life – but he doesn't know this. `1.1`
- Macbeth thinks he is safe because Birnam Wood can't move to Dunsinane – but he has misunderstood the double meaning of the apparitions. That's irony. `5.5`
- Lady Macbeth thinks a little water will clear the blood from her hands – but the spot remains to haunt her. That too is irony! `5.1`

 *Discuss... **irony***

Can you find other examples of dramatic or verbal irony? Here are some clues to start you off:

- Duncan's arrival at Macbeth's castle. `1.6`
- The porter's references to hell. `2.3`
- At the banquet, Macbeth drinking to 'our dear friend Banquo, whom we miss'. `3.4`
- The second apparition saying, 'none of woman born/ Shall harm Macbeth'. `4.1`

 *Discuss... **other dramatic techniques***

1. **Comic relief.** Shakespeare had to please a very mixed audience and he usually introduced some comedy into his tragedies to lighten the heavy mood. Where in *Macbeth* has he done this? Do you think it is simply comedy, or is there more to it?
2. **Soliloquies.** We have seen how effective soliloquies are in taking us into a character's inner thoughts. How do you think a soliloquy ought to be delivered in the theatre? Does the actor speak quietly to himself or herself, or directly to the audience? `p20`
3. **The supernatural.** Discuss how you bring out the drama of one of the 'supernatural' scenes in the play through the use of lighting, music, special effects and stage design.
4. **Scenes of action.** Towards the end of the play there are several scenes of action, particularly sword fights. Do they make good drama? How would you stage them?

Shakespeare and NCTs

Assessment Objectives

Your Shakespeare paper is part of your National Curriculum Tests. It is designed to test your ability to understand and respond to:

- Shakespeare's presentation of ideas
- The motivation and behaviour of characters
- The development of plot
- The language of the scenes
- The overall impact of the scenes
- The presentation of the scenes on stage.

You will also be assessed on the quality of your writing.

In the exam you will be asked a question on a scene which you have studied beforehand, but you will be expected to relate this scene to the play as a whole.

Probably the most important, and difficult, thing to remember in your exam is that you are writing about a play, not just words on a page. Some questions in the exam remind you of this, and ask for things like advice to actors, or your views if you were a director, but this very important fact should be at the back of your mind in any answer you attempt.

Shakespeare's presentation of ideas Shakespeare developed his ideas, or themes, through both the plot and the language of the play. But remember that he was writing for the theatre. In getting an idea across he would have had to consider how it would work on the stage.

The motivation and behaviour of characters The behaviour of characters – what they say and do – is relatively easy to see and to comment on. A character's motivation (why they behave as they do) can only be judged by assessing the character throughout the play. You can then relate their motivation to their actions in the scene you are writing about.

The development of plot You can only really understand the scene you have been given if you know how it fits into the action of the play as a whole. Is it:

- developing the plot
- a major crisis in the play itself
- building up tension
- raising a smile
- advancing our understanding of the characters?

The language of the scene You will have spent time before the exam looking at the language of the scene that has been set. Understanding the language, therefore, should not be a problem. What you need to discuss is the effect of the language on the characters in the scene and on the audience.

The overall impact of the scene To get the best marks you need to be able to discuss how your scene works on all its different levels, including how it might affect the audience.

The presentation of the scene on stage You need to be able to express ideas on how the script might be brought to life by real actors on a real stage.

REMEMBER You will also be assessed on the quality of your writing, so it is important to write clearly, using the correct vocabulary, spelling and punctuation.

How to do well in your Shakespeare paper

- Read the whole play at least once.
- Go and see a production of the play.
- Watch film versions of the play.
- Act out your set scene.
- Know your set scene really well. Make sure you know the meaning of all the words.
- Know how your scene fits into the play as a whole.
- Have a good idea of what Shakespeare is trying to do in your set scene.
- Practise writing under timed conditions.

Using quotations and evidence

When you are writing about a scene you need to provide evidence for the examiner. The best way of doing this is to refer closely to the text or to provide a quotation.

'Referring closely to the text' does not mean retelling what is happening in your chosen scene. Instead, quotations should be used to back up and support your comments. For example:

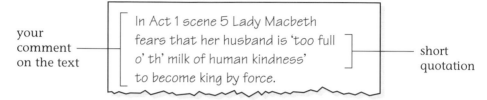

your comment on the text

In Act 1 scene 5 Lady Macbeth fears that her husband is 'too full o' th' milk of human kindness' to become king by force.

short quotation

Note that short quotations are inside inverted commas and on the same line as the rest of your writing. Longer quotations are laid out exactly as you find them in the play, but if there is only one person speaking, it is not necessary to give the name. You can make your comment before or after the quotation.

Sample questions

Below are some examples of the kind of questions you will meet in your Shakespeare paper. They all relate to *Macbeth*.

Act 4 scene 1

TASK 1

In this scene Macbeth returns to the witches to find out more about his future.

How do Macbeth's attitude to and feelings about the witches and the apparitions change through Act 4 scene 1?

Before you begin to write you should think about:

- how Macbeth speaks to the witches through the scene;
- Macbeth's reactions to the different apparitions;
- Macbeth's thoughts and feelings at the end of the scene.

Read the task again before you begin to write your answer.

Before writing your answer to Task 1, you should make notes on the bullet points above and select appropriate quotations. Your notes may look like the following:

- Through the scene Macbeth is constantly demanding answers from the witches – he even threatens them when they at first refuse to answer his questions about Banquo's 'issue' becoming kings. Macbeth is quite insulting to the witches – calls them 'secret, black, and midnight hags'. The way he relates to them emphasizes his arrogance. His foolishness/blindness is an example of dramatic irony – by the end we know that the witches have deceived him, when we see the outcome of the prophecies.

- Macbeth has different reactions to the different apparitions. 'Armed Head': confirms his fears about Macduff – he wants to know more but is prevented. 'Bloody Child': Macbeth is partly relieved since it seems he cannot be harmed by any 'of woman born'; yet he doesn't seem entirely convinced since he decides to destroy Macduff anyway, to 'make assurance double sure'. 'A Child Crowned': again Macbeth seems relieved ('sweet bodements, good!') since it would appear impossible for Birnam Wood to march towards his castle – but Macbeth wants to know even more. 'A Show of eight Kings': this apparition unsettles Macbeth, as it is not what he wants to see ('Thy crown does sear mine eye-balls') – once again it means his future is uncertain and threatened.

- Conclusion: At the beginning of the scene Macbeth is determined to have answers; he is forthright and acts arrogantly. But his feelings change throughout this scene. Sometimes he feels reassured but ultimately he is troubled and insecure – the prophecies don't put his mind at ease. He treats the witches almost with contempt, but he is shaken by the apparitions that they show him. By the end he curses himself for trusting them – 'And damn'd all those that trust them!' He decides to act on his feelings without thinking – 'The very firstlings of my heart shall be the firstlings of my hand' – to seize Macduff's castle and murder his family. Although he seems determined and strong here, he is also acting out of his insecurities.

 *Write... **answers to sample questions***

Look at Tasks 2 and 3 on page 48. Write your answers in note form, in a similar way to the notes above. Choose one of these tasks and, as homework, write up the notes as a full answer. Remember to write clearly, using the correct vocabulary, spelling and punctuation.

p48

Act 1 scene 4 to Act 1 scene 5 up to the entrance of Macbeth ('To cry "Hold, hold!"')

TASK 2

In Act 1 scene 4 Macbeth has an audience with King Duncan. In the following scene Lady Macbeth reads the letter her husband has sent her telling of the witches' prophecies.

Explain in detail how Shakespeare portrays the characters in these two scenes and creates dramatic tension.

Before you begin to write you should think about:

In Act 1 scene 4:
- what Duncan says at the beginning about the first Thane of Cawdor and the way he treats Macbeth;
- what Macbeth says to Duncan before Malcolm is announced heir to the throne;
- the way Macbeth acts after Malcolm is made the king's successor;
- the different ways in which Macbeth speaks in the scene.

In Act 1 scene 5, up to the entrance of Macbeth:
- what Lady Macbeth is determined will happen;
- Macbeth's character, as revealed in Lady Macbeth's words;
- how she intends to influence Macbeth;
- the kind of language and imagery she uses.

Read the task again before you begin to write your answer.

Act 3 scene 4

TASK 3

In this scene Macbeth holds a banquet for his lords, during which he sees the ghost of Banquo.

Imagine that you are Lady Macbeth. Write down your thoughts and feelings about your husband's behaviour at the banquet.

Before you begin you should think about:
- the way Macbeth behaves when speaking to the stranger at the door (the murderer);
- how he behaves towards the lords at the start;
- how Macbeth's attitude and behaviour changes when he sees the ghost;
- how you felt and what you said and did to calm the situation;
- the way Macbeth's character seems to have changed by the end.

Read the task again before you begin to write your answer.